VITAMIN A-Z
NO MORE SUPPLEMENTS

THE NATURAL FOOD GUIDE TO PROMOTE A HEALTHY LIFESTYLE WITH VITAMINS, NUTRIENTS AND MINERALS FROM NOURISHIING FOODS.

SHANE RAYMOND

2

Copyright © 2023 by Shane Raymond

3

TABLE OF CONTENTS

INTRODUCTION

There was a young child named Sally who lived in a place where there were plenty of fruits, vegetables, and other wholesome foods. Sally enjoyed eating a wide range of delectable meals and playing outside with her friends. She was unaware of the significance of vitamins for her body, though.

Sally began to feel weak and exhausted one day. Upon noticing her diminished energy levels, her friends made the decision to assist her. They took Sally to see the knowledgeable elderly herbalist, who informed them that vitamins were what kept Sally robust and well.

Sally learned about the various kinds of vitamins and their functions in the body from the herbalist. For instance, vitamin C supports the upkeep of a healthy immune system and encourage the development of robust teeth and bones. In contrast, vitamin D facilitates the absorption of calcium and phosphorus, both of which are necessary for healthy bones.

Sally made the decision to alter her diet after being astounded by the information she learned. She started consuming more vitamin-rich fruits and vegetables, and soon she started feeling better. She had more energy and could play with her friends once more.

RELATIONSHIP BETWEEN VITAMINS, NUTRIENTS AND MINERALS

Vitamins, nutrients, and minerals are essential components of a healthy diet, as they play crucial roles in maintaining the overall well-being of an individual. These micronutrients are responsible for a variety of functions within the body, including supporting the immune system, promoting growth and development, and ensuring proper functioning of organs and systems. In this essay, we will discuss the importance of vitamins, nutrients, and minerals and their role in maintaining a healthy body.

Vitamins

Organic substances called vitamins are necessary for the body to function properly in little amounts. The two categories of vitamins are fat-soluble and water-soluble. Fat-soluble vitamins (A, D, E, and K) are stored in the body's fat tissues, while water-soluble vitamins (B complex and C) are easily absorbed and excreted by the body.

Vitamins play a vital role in various bodily processes, such as supporting the immune system, maintaining healthy skin, and ensuring proper functioning of the nervous and muscular systems. A deficiency in vitamins can lead to health problems, such as anemia, weakened immune system, and poor bone health.

Nutrients

Nutrients are the essential components of food that provide energy, support growth, and maintain overall health. There are six main classes of nutrients: carbohydrates, proteins, fats, fiber, vitamins, and minerals. These nutrients are necessary for the proper functioning of the body's organs, tissues, and cells. Carbohydrates, proteins, and fats are macronutrients, which provide the body with energy. Fiber, on the other hand, aids in digestion and helps maintain a healthy gut. Nutrients play a critical role in maintaining the body's metabolism, immune system, and overall health.

Minerals

Inorganic materials called minerals are essential to the body's healthy operation. The two categories for which they are categorized are macrominerals and trace minerals. Macro-minerals, such as calcium, magnesium, phosphorus, and potassium, are required in larger amounts, while trace minerals, such as iron, zinc, and iodine, are needed in smaller amounts. Minerals play a vital role in various bodily processes, such as maintaining bone health, supporting muscle function, and ensuring proper fluid balance. A deficiency in minerals can lead to health problems, such as anemia, weak bones, and poor nerve function.

COMMON NUTRITION MYTHS AND MISCONCEPTIONS

There are numerous myths and misconceptions surrounding food and nutrition that have been perpetuated over the years. These myths often lead to confusion and misinformation about what constitutes a healthy diet. It is essential to debunk these myths and provide accurate information to promote better understanding of nutrition.

Myth 1: Carbohydrates are Unhealthy

One common misconception is that carbohydrates are inherently unhealthy and should be avoided. While it is true that excessive consumption of refined carbohydrates can lead to health issues such as obesity and diabetes, not all carbohydrates are bad. In fact, carbohydrates are the body's primary source of energy, and they are essential for proper bodily functions. The key lies in consuming complex carbohydrates such as whole grains, fruits, and vegetables, which provide essential nutrients and fiber.

Myth 2: It's Bad for You to Eat Any Fat

Another prevalent myth is the demonization of all fats. While it is important to limit the intake of trans fats and saturated fats, certain types of fats are actually beneficial for health. Unsaturated fats, such as those found in avocados, nuts, and olive oil, can have positive effects on heart health when consumed in moderation. Omega-3 fatty acids, in particular, play a crucial role in brain function and reducing the risk of cardiovascular disease.

Myth 3: You Can Lose Weight by Skipping Meals

Many people think that eating less is possible when missing meals. However, this approach can be counterproductive. When individuals skip meals, they often end up overeating later in the day or making unhealthy food choices due to increased hunger. Additionally, skipping meals can lead to a decrease in energy levels and nutrient deficiencies. Instead of skipping meals, focusing on portion control and consuming a balanced diet is a more sustainable approach to weight management.

Myth 4: All Protein Supplements are Beneficial

The widespread belief that all protein supplements are beneficial for health is also a misconception. While protein is an essential macronutrient for muscle repair and growth, relying solely on protein supplements can lead to an imbalance in nutrient intake. Whole food sources of protein such as lean meats, fish, eggs, dairy products, legumes, and nuts offer a wider array of nutrients along with protein.

Myth 5: Compared to added sugar, natural sugar is healthier

There is a common belief that natural sugars found in fruits are healthier than added sugars found in processed foods. While it is true that natural sugars come with additional nutrients and fiber, excessive consumption of natural sugars can still contribute to an increase in calorie intake. Moderation is key when it comes to all types of sugar consumption.

Myth 6: Organic Foods Are Always Healthier

The perception that organic foods are always healthier than conventionally grown foods is another prevalent myth. While organic produce may reduce exposure to pesticides, it does not automatically make them more nutritious. Both organic and conventional produce can be part of a healthy diet, and the most important factor is consuming a variety of fruits and vegetables.

In conclusion, debunking common nutrition myths and misconceptions is crucial for promoting accurate information about food and nutrition. By addressing these misconceptions with evidence-based knowledge, individuals can make informed decisions about their dietary choices.

WHAT IS VITAMIN?

Vitamins are essential micronutrients that our body requires in small amounts to function properly. They play a crucial role in various biological processes, including growth, development, and overall health maintenance. There are two types of vitamins: water-soluble and fat-soluble. Fat-soluble vitamins (A, D, E, and K) can be stored in the body's fat tissue, while water-soluble vitamins (B and C) are easily absorbed and quickly eliminated from the body.
Vitamins are naturally occurring in a variety of foods, such as fruits, vegetables, and animal products. They can also be obtained through supplements, although it is generally recommended to get them from a balanced diet. A deficiency in any of these essential nutrients can lead to health problems, while an excess can cause toxicity.

Vitamins perform several vital functions in the body, including:

1. Regulating metabolism: Vitamins play a crucial role in breaking down carbohydrates, proteins, and fats for energy production.
2. Supporting immune function: Vitamins help the immune system fight infections and diseases by maintaining the integrity of the

    skin, mucous membranes, and other barriers that protect the body from harmful pathogens.

3. Maintaining healthy skin and hair: Vitamins A, C, and E contribute to the health and appearance of the skin, hair, and nails.
4. Bone growth and maintenance: Vitamin D, in conjunction with calcium, helps build and maintain strong bones.
5. Blood clotting: Vitamin K is essential for proper blood clotting, which is crucial for preventing excessive bleeding.
6. Nervous system function: Vitamins B1, B6, B12, and niacin play a role in maintaining the health of the nervous system, including the brain.
7. Red blood cell formation: Folate (folic acid) and vitamin B12 are necessary for the production of red blood cells, which transport oxygen throughout the body.

Vitamin deficiencies can lead to various health problems, such as anemia, weakened immune system, poor growth, and developmental issues. In contrast, excessive intake of certain vitamins can result in toxicity, which can cause symptoms such as nausea, vomiting, diarrhea, and even organ damage.

It is important to maintain a balanced diet and consult a healthcare professional before taking supplements to ensure that the appropriate amounts of vitamins are consumed.

WATER-SOLUBLE VITAMINS

Vitamin B

Vitamin B is a group of essential nutrients that play a crucial role in maintaining overall health and well-being. There are eight B vitamins, each with its own specific functions and benefits for the body. These vitamins are water-soluble, meaning they are not stored in the body and need to be consumed regularly through a balanced diet or supplements.

***Vitamin B** consists of several different B vitamins including*
- *B1 (thiamine)*
- *B2 (riboflavin)*
- *B3 (niacin)*
- *B5 (pantothenic acid)*
- *B6 (pyridoxine)*
- *B7 (biotin)*
- *B9 (folic acid), and*
- *B12 (cobalamin). Each has its own functions, benefits, examples, etc.*

Vitamin B1 (Thiamine):

- **Importance:** Supports the nervous system and energy metabolism.
- **Functions:** Converts carbohydrates into glucose, which is then used as energy.
- **Benefits:** Promotes healthy nerve function and brain development.
- **Examples:** Whole grains, legumes, pork, and fortified cereals.
- **Description:** Water-soluble vitamin involved in energy production and nerve function.
- **Role in the body:** Thiamine helps convert carbohydrates into glucose, which is used for energy.
- **Side effects:** Rarely observed, but excessive intake may cause stomach upset.
- **Warnings:** Deficiency can lead to symptoms like weight loss, fatigue, and irritability.
- **Precautions:** Individuals with alcohol dependence may require higher intakes.
- **Signs of deficiency:** Beriberi, Wernicke-Korsakoff syndrome.

- ○ **Amount needed in the body:** Adult males require 1.2 mg/day, females require 1.1 mg/day.
- ○ **Best way to consume:** Include whole grains, legumes, and fortified cereals in the diet.

Recipe 1

Quinoa salad

Ingredients: 1 cup cooked quinoa, 1/2 cup cherry tomatoes (halved), 1/4 cup cucumber (diced), 1/4 cup red onion (chopped), 2 tablespoons fresh parsley (chopped), 2 tablespoons lemon juice, 1 tablespoon olive oil, salt, pepper.

Instructions: In a bowl, combine the cooked quinoa, cherry tomatoes, cucumber, red onion, and parsley. Whisk the olive oil and lemon juice in a separate small bowl. After adding the dressing, mix the quinoa salad to incorporate. Season with salt and pepper to taste.

Recipe 2

Ingredients for the Vitamin B1 (Thiamine)
- 1 cup entire grain or sustained cereal
- 1/2 cup earthy colored rice
- 1/4 cup dried beans or peas
- 1/4 cup dried natural product
- 1/4 cup nuts or seeds
- 1/2 teaspoon salt
- 1/4 teaspoon dark pepper
- 1/4 teaspoon cayenne pepper (discretionary)

Directions:

1. Start by washing and depleting the beans and peas.
2. In a huge pot, join the entire grain or braced oat, earthy colored rice, beans or peas, dried natural product, nuts or seeds, salt, dark pepper, and cayenne pepper (if utilizing).
3. The proportion of water to grain or cereal mixture in the pot should be 2 cups for every 1 cup of water.
4. Heat the blend to the point of boiling, then, at that point, lessen the intensity to a stew.

5.   Cover the pot and let it cook for around 45 minutes to 60 minutes, or until the grains, rice, and beans are delicate.

6.   Mix every so often to guarantee in any event, cooking.

7.   Once cooked, eliminate from intensity and let it represent a couple of moments prior to serving.

The body needs vitamin B1, also known as thiamine, to convert carbohydrates into glucose, which is needed to produce energy. This vital nutrient is abundant in whole grains, fortified cereals, beans, peas, dried fruit, nuts, and seeds.

o   **Normal food sources (creature based)**: Beef liver, pork.

Natural (non-animal) sources of food: Seeds, nuts (such as almonds), legumes (such as beans and lentils), and whole grains (such as rice and oats)

2.   **Vitamin B2 (Riboflavin):**
•Importance: Upholds the development, capability, and support of cells.

o   **Benefits:** It assumes a key part in energy digestion, helping convert starches, fats, and proteins into usable energy. Riboflavin additionally goes about as a cancer prevention agent, shielding cells from oxidative harm.

•**Description:** Advances solid skin, eyes, and red platelet arrangement.
○**Examples:** Dairy items, eggs, lean meats, and invigorated oats.
○**Importance:** Because it is a water-soluble vitamin, the body does not store a large amount of riboflavin, so it must be replenished frequently through diet or supplements.

 Function in the body: Carbohydrate, fat, and protein metabolism all depend on riboflavin.
○   **Side effects:** When taken in the right amounts, riboflavin is generally regarded as safe and does not cause significant side effects. It might cause innocuous yellow staining of pee.

○   **Warning:** Skin conditions, mouth lesions, and anemia are all signs of deficiency.
○   **Precautions:** Riboflavin supplementation or higher doses may be required by those with certain genetic disorders or conditions that affect nutrient absorption.

Signs of Deficiency: Breaks and wounds around the sides of the mouth, enlarged or sore tongue, skin rash, aversion to light.

 The amount required by the body: Grown-up guys require 1.3 mg/day, females require 1.1 mg/day.

The best way to eat: A well-balanced diet rich in dairy products, lean meats, eggs, leafy green vegetables, and fortified cereals can provide riboflavin.

Recipe:

Omelette with spinach and feta - Ingredients: 3 huge eggs, 1/4 cup disintegrated feta cheddar, 1 cup new spinach (slashed), 1/4 teaspoon dried oregano, salt, pepper, olive oil.

Instructions: In a bowl, beat the eggs until very much blended. Mix in the feta cheddar, spinach, dried oregano, salt, and pepper. Heat a little non-stick skillet over medium intensity and add a shower of olive oil. Empty the egg blend into the skillet and cook until the edges begin to set. Use a spatula to gently lift the omelette's edges and tilt the skillet to let any uncooked eggs flow to the edges. Fold the omelette in half after it has mostly set and cook for another minute or until it is cooked through.

- ○ **Regular food sources** (creature based): Yogurt, milk, and eggs.
- ○ **Normal food sources** (non-creature based): Verdant green vegetables (spinach, kale), mushrooms, almonds.

Vitamin B3 (Niacin):

- ○ **Importance:** Supports healthy skin, nerves, and digestive system.
- ○ **Functions:** Converts food into energy and helps maintain healthy skin and nerves.
- ○ **Benefits:** Regulates cholesterol levels and prevents cardiovascular disease.
- ○ **Examples:** Meat, poultry, fish, peanuts, and fortified cereals.
- ○ **Description:** Water-soluble vitamin involved in energy metabolism and cellular function.

- **Role in the body:** Niacin is involved in the metabolism of carbohydrates, fats, and proteins.
- **Side effects:** High doses may cause flushing, itching, and liver damage.
- **Warnings:** Deficiency can lead to symptoms like pellagra, skin disorders, and mental confusion.
- **Precautions:** Individuals with liver or kidney disease may require reduced intake.
- **Signs of deficiency:** Skin issues, mental confusion, and gastrointestinal problems.
- **Amount needed in the body:** Adult males require 16 mg/day, females require 14 mg/day.
- **Best way to consume:** Include meat, poultry, fish, peanuts, and fortified cereals in the diet.

Recipe

Ingredients:

- 1 cup whole wheat flour
- 1/2 cup all-purpose flour
- 1/4 cup rolled oats
- 1/4 cup almonds, chopped
- 1/4 cup sunflower seeds
- 1/4 cup pumpkin seeds
- 1/4 cup raisins
- 1/4 cup dried cranberries
- 1/4 cup coconut oil, melted
- 1/4 cup honey
- 1 teaspoon cinnamon
- 1/2 teaspoon baking soda
- 1/4 teaspoon salt
- 1/4 teaspoon Vitamin B3 (Niacin) supplement (optional)

Instructions:

1. Preheat your oven to 350°F (175°C).
2. In a large bowl, mix together the whole wheat flour, all-purpose flour, rolled oats, chopped almonds, sunflower seeds, pumpkin seeds, raisins, and dried cranberries.
3. In a separate bowl, whisk together the melted coconut oil, honey, cinnamon, baking soda, salt, and Vitamin B3 supplement (if using).

4. Add the liquid mixture to the dry mixture and stir until thoroughly blended.
5. Line a baking sheet with parchment paper and drop spoonfuls of the dough onto the sheet, leaving some space between each one.
6. Bake for 12-15 minutes, or until the edges are golden brown.
7. Take the cookies out of the oven and allow them to cool for a few minutes on the baking sheet before moving them to a wire rack to finish cooling.

Enjoy your Vitamin B3-rich cookies as a healthy snack or breakfast option.

- **Natural food sources:** Meat, poultry, fish, peanuts, fortified cereals, and whole grains.

Vitamin B5 (Pantothenic Acid):

- **Importance:** Supports healthy skin, hair, and nerves.
- **Functions:** Involved in energy production and fatty acid synthesis.
- **Benefits:** Regulates stress hormones and supports adrenal function.

- o **Examples:** Meat, poultry, fish, eggs, and fortified cereals.
- o **Description:** Water-soluble vitamin involved in energy metabolism and cellular function.
- o **Role in the body:** Pantothenic acid is involved in the synthesis of coenzyme A, which plays a role in energy production.
- o **Side effects:** Rare, but excessive intake may cause stomach upset.
- o **Warnings:** Deficiency can lead to fatigue, irritability, and gastrointestinal issues.
- o **Precautions:** No known precautions.
- o **Signs of deficiency:** Fatigue, irritability, and gastrointestinal problems.
- o **Amount needed in the body:** Adult males require 5 mg/day, females require 4 mg/day.
- o **Best way to consume:** Include meat, poultry, fish, eggs, and fortified cereals in the diet.

Recipe

Pantothenic acid-rich Recipe:

Ingredients:
1. **Whole grains:** Whole grains such as brown rice, whole wheat, and oats are rich sources of vitamin B5.
2. **Meat:** Chicken, beef, and pork are excellent sources of vitamin B5.
3. **Fish:** Tuna, salmon, and other types of fish contain high levels of vitamin B5.
4. **Eggs:** Eggs are a good source of vitamin B5.
5. **Dairy products:** Milk, yogurt, and cheese are rich in vitamin B5.
6. **Legumes:** Lentils, chickpeas, and split peas are good plant-based sources of vitamin B5.
7. **Avocado:** Avocado is a fruit that contains a significant amount of vitamin B5.
8. **Mushrooms:** Certain types of mushrooms, such as shiitake mushrooms, are a source of vitamin B5.

Note: There isn't a specific recipe for obtaining vitamin B5 as it is naturally present in a wide variety of foods. However, incorporating the aforementioned ingredients into one's diet can help ensure an adequate intake of vitamin B5.

- **Natural food sources:** Meat, poultry, fish, eggs, fortified cereals, and whole grains.

Vitamin B6 (Pyridoxine):

- **Importance:** Supports healthy brain function, immune system, and red blood cell formation.
- **Functions:** Involved in the metabolism of proteins, fats, and carbohydrates.
- **Benefits:** Regulates homocysteine levels, which reduces the risk of heart disease.
- **Examples:** Meat, poultry, fish, bananas, and fortified cereals.
- **Description:** Water-soluble vitamin involved in energy metabolism and cellular function.
- **Role in the body:** Pyridoxine is involved in the metabolism of proteins, fats, and carbohydrates.
- **Side effects:** Rare, but excessive intake may cause stomach upset.

- o **Warnings:** Deficiency can lead to anemia, weakened immune system, and impaired cognitive function.
- o **Precautions:** Individuals with kidney disease may require reduced intake.
- o **Signs of deficiency:** Anemia, weakened immune system, and impaired cognitive function.
- o **Amount needed in the body:** Adult males require 1.3 mg/day, females require 1.3 mg/day.
- o **Best way to consume:** Include meat, poultry, fish, bananas, and fortified cereals in the diet.

Recipe

Vitamin B6 (Pyridoxine) Recipe

Ingredients
- 1 lb. Chicken breasts without the bones and skin, sliced into little pieces
- 2 cups mixed vegetables (such as bell peppers, onions, and mushrooms)
- 2 tbsp. olive oil
- 2 cloves garlic, minced

- 2 tbsp. soy sauce
- 1 tbsp. honey
- 1 tbsp. rice vinegar
- 1 tsp. sesame oil
- 1/2 tsp. ground ginger
- 1/4 tsp. black pepper
- 1/4 tsp. red pepper flakes (optional)
- Cooked brown rice, for serving

Instructions:

1. In a small bowl, whisk together the soy sauce, honey, rice vinegar, sesame oil, ground ginger, black pepper, and red pepper flakes (if using). Set aside.
2. In a large skillet or wok, heat the olive oil over medium-high heat. Add the chicken and heat for 5 to 7 minutes, or until browned and cooked through. Remove from the pan and set aside.
3. Add the mixed vegetables to the skillet and cook until they are tender-crisp, about 3-4 minutes.
4. Return the chicken to the skillet and add the sauce. Stir to coat the chicken and vegetables evenly.
5. Serve the stir-fry over cooked brown rice.

   - **Natural food sources:** Meat, poultry, fish, bananas, fortified cereals, and whole grains.

Vitamin B7 (Biotin):

Vitamin B7, also known as biotin, is a water-soluble vitamin that plays a crucial role in various metabolic processes in the body, including the metabolism of fats, carbohydrates, and proteins. It is also essential for the health of the skin, hair, and nails. While biotin can be obtained through supplements, it is also naturally found in a variety of foods.

- **Importance:** Supports healthy hair, skin, and nails.
- **Functions:** Involved in fatty acid synthesis and energy metabolism.
- **Benefits:** Regulates blood sugar levels and supports pregnant women's health.
- **Examples:** Eggs, nuts, seeds, and some fruits.
- **Description:** Water-soluble vitamin involved in energy metabolism and cellular function.
- **Role in the body:** Biotin is involved in the metabolism of carbohydrates, fats, and proteins.
- **Side effects:** Rare, but excessive intake may cause stomach upset.
- **Warnings:** Deficiency is rare, but it can lead to hair loss, skin rashes, and nerve damage.

- o **Precautions:** No known precautions.
- o **Signs of deficiency:** Hair loss, skin rashes, and nerve damage.
- o **Amount needed in the body:** Adult males require 2.5 mg/day, females require 2.5 mg/day.
- o **Best way to consume:** Include eggs, nuts, seeds, and some fruits in the diet.

Recipies

Egg Yolks
- **Ingredients**: Eggs
- **Description**:
  - o Crack open the eggs, then take out the yolks and whites.
  - o The egg yolks can be used in various recipes such as omelets, scrambled eggs, or as an ingredient in baked goods like cakes and custards.

Nuts and Seeds
- **Ingredients**: Almonds, Walnuts, Sunflower seeds
- **Description**:
  - o Almonds:
    - Enjoy a handful of almonds as a snack.

- - Incorporate almonds into salads or use them as a topping for yogurt or oatmeal.
  - Walnuts:
    - - Add walnuts to your breakfast cereal or oatmeal.
      - Use walnuts in baking recipes such as banana bread or muffins.
  - Sunflower seeds:
    - - Sprinkle sunflower seeds on top of salads or soups.
      - Blend sunflower seeds into homemade pesto for a nutritious boost.

Sweet Potatoes
- **Ingredients**: Sweet potatoes
- **Description**:
  - Roast sweet potatoes in the oven with a drizzle of olive oil and your choice of seasonings.
  - Mash cooked sweet potatoes and serve as a side dish or use them as an ingredient in soups and stews.

Spinach
- **Ingredients**: Spinach
- **Description**:
  - Prepare a fresh spinach salad with added vegetables and your choice of protein such as grilled chicken or tofu.

- ○ Sauté spinach with garlic and olive oil for a simple yet nutritious side dish.

Whole Grains
- **Ingredients**: Quinoa, Oats
- **Description**:
  - ○ Quinoa:
    - Cook quinoa according to package instructions and use it as a base for grain bowls or salads.
    - Incorporate quinoa into stuffed bell peppers or use it as a filling for vegetarian wraps.
  - ○ Oats:
    - Prepare oatmeal for breakfast topped with fruits, nuts, and a drizzle of honey.
    - Use oats in homemade granola bars or cookies for a wholesome treat.

  - ○ **Natural food sources:** Eggs, nuts, seeds, and some fruits.

Vitamin B9 (Folate):

- **Importance:** Supports healthy fetal development, red blood cell formation, and immune function.
- **Functions:** Involved in DNA synthesis and cell division.
- **Benefits:** Regulates homocysteine levels, which reduces the risk of heart disease.
- **Examples:** Leafy green vegetables, legumes, and fortified cereals.
- **Description:** Water-soluble vitamin involved in DNA synthesis and cellular function.
- **Role in the body:** Folate is involved in the synthesis of DNA and the formation of red blood cells.
- **Side effects:** Rare, but excessive intake may cause stomach upset.
- **Warnings:** Deficiency can lead to anemia, birth defects, and impaired immune function.
- **Precautions:** Individuals with kidney disease may require reduced intake.
- **Signs of deficiency:** Anemia, birth defects, and impaired immune function.

- ○ **Amount needed in the body:** Adult males require 400 mcg/day, females require 400 mcg/day.
- ○ **Best way to consume:** Include leafy green vegetables, legumes, and fortified cereals in the diet.

Recipe

Folate-rich recipe Spinach and Chickpea Salad with Lemon Dressing

Ingredients:
- 2 cups of fresh spinach leaves
- 1 cup of cooked chickpeas
- 1/4 cup of diced red onion
- 1/4 cup of crumbled feta cheese
- 2 tablespoons of olive oil
- 1 tablespoon of lemon juice
- Salt and pepper to taste

Instructions:
1. In a large bowl, combine the spinach, chickpeas, red onion, and feta cheese.
2. In a small bowl, mix the olive oil, lemon juice, salt, and pepper to make the dressing.

3. Drizzle the salad with the dressing and toss to evenly coat.

4. Serve immediately and enjoy this nutritious and folate-rich salad.

Natural food sources: Leafy green vegetables, legumes, fortified cereals, and whole grains.

Vitamin B12 (Cobalamin):

Vitamin B12, also known as Cobalamin, is an essential nutrient that plays a critical role in the normal functioning of the brain and nervous system, as well as the formation of red blood cells. It is important to include foods rich in Vitamin B12 in your diet to maintain overall health. Here are three recipes that incorporate Vitamin B12-rich ingredients

- o **Importance:** Supports healthy nerve function, red blood cell formation, and DNA synthesis.
- o **Functions:** Involved in the metabolism of proteins, fats, and carbohydrates.

- **Benefits:** Regulates homocysteine levels, which reduces the risk of heart disease.
- **Examples:** Animal products, fortified cereals, and nutritional yeast.
- **Description:** Water-soluble vitamin involved in energy metabolism and cellular function.
- **Role in the body:** Cobalamin is involved in the metabolism of proteins, fats, and carbohydrates.
- **Side effects:** Rare, but excessive intake may cause stomach upset.
- **Warnings:** Deficiency can lead to anemia, nerve damage, and impaired immune function.
- **Precautions:** Individuals with kidney disease may require reduced intake.
- **Signs of deficiency:** Anemia, nerve damage, and impaired immune function.
- **Amount needed in the body:** Adult males require 2.4 mcg/day, females require 2.4 mcg/day.
- **Best way to consume:** Include animal products, fortified cereals, and nutritional yeast in the diet.

Recipe

Vitamin B12-rich

Beef and Mushroom Stir-Fry

Ingredients:
- 1 lb lean beef, sliced
- 1 lb mixed mushrooms, sliced
- 1 onion, chopped
- 3 cloves garlic, minced
- 1 tbsp olive oil
- 1/4 cup low-sodium soy sauce
- 2 tbsp Worcestershire sauce
- 1 tbsp rice vinegar
- 1 tsp sesame oil
- Salt and pepper, to taste

Instructions:
1. In a large skillet or wok, heat olive oil over medium-high heat. Add the onion and simmer for about 3 minutes, or until softened.
2. Add the garlic and cook for another minute until fragrant.
3. Add the beef and mushrooms to the skillet, stirring occasionally until the beef is browned and the mushrooms are tender.

4. In a small bowl, whisk together the soy sauce, Worcestershire sauce, rice vinegar, and sesame oil.
5. Pour the sauce over the beef and mushrooms, stirring to coat evenly.
6. Add pepper and salt to taste.
7. Serve over rice or noodles.

This recipe is rich in Vitamin B12 due to the beef and mushrooms, which are both excellent sources of the nutrient.

> **Natural food sources:** Animal products, fortified cereals, and nutritional yeast.

FAT-SOLUBLE VITAMINS

Vitamin A

Vitamin A is essential for immune system support, healthy vision maintenance, and appropriate growth and development.

- **Functions:** Vitamin A is essential for vision, immune function, and reproduction. It also plays a role in the normal functioning of the heart, lungs, kidneys, and other organs.
- **Benefits:** Supports healthy vision, boosts the immune system, promotes cell growth and differentiation.
- **Examples:** Retinol, retinal, retinoic acid.
- **Description:** Vitamin A is a fat-soluble vitamin that exists in several forms. Retinol, retinal, and retinoic acid are active forms of vitamin A found in animal-based foods. Beta-carotene is a provitamin A carotenoid found in plants which can be converted into vitamin A in the body.

- **Role in the Body:** It plays a vital role in maintaining healthy vision, ensuring the normal functioning of the immune system, and supporting cell growth and differentiation.

- **Side Effects:** Excessive intake of vitamin A can lead to toxicity symptoms such as nausea, dizziness, and even liver damage.
- **Warnings:** Pregnant women should avoid excessive vitamin A intake as it may harm the developing fetus. Individuals with liver disease or other health conditions should consult a healthcare professional before taking high doses of vitamin A supplements.

- **Precautions:** The recommended daily allowance (RDA) for vitamin A varies depending on age and gender. It is important to meet but not exceed the recommended intake levels.

- **Signs of Deficiency:** Night blindness (difficulty seeing in low-light conditions), dry eyes, increased susceptibility to infections, dry skin, poor wound healing.

- **Amount You Need in the Body:** The recommended dietary allowance (RDA) for vitamin A is 900 micrograms per day for men and 700 micrograms per day for women.

- **Best Way to Consume:** Vitamin A can be obtained through a balanced diet that includes animal-based sources like liver, fish, and dairy products, as well as plant-based sources like carrots, sweet potatoes, and leafy green vegetables.

- **Recipe:** Carrot and sweet potato soup - Ingredients: 2 large carrots, 1 large sweet potato, 1 onion, 2 cloves of garlic, vegetable broth, salt, pepper. Instructions: Peel and chop the carrots, sweet potato, onion, and garlic. Add the onion and garlic to a pot and cook until transparent. Add the carrots and sweet potato and cook for a few minutes. Pour in enough vegetable broth to cover the vegetables. Simmer until the vegetables are tender. Puree the soup using an immersion blender or blender until it's smooth. Season with salt and pepper to taste.

- **Natural Food Sources:**
    - Natural food sources (animal-based): Liver (beef, chicken), fish (salmon, mackerel), dairy products (milk, cheese).
    - Natural food sources (non-animal-based): Carrots, sweet potatoes, spinach, kale.

Vitamin C

Vitamin C is a water-soluble vitamin that plays crucial roles in various bodily functions. It is essential for the growth, development, and repair of tissues.

Vitamin C (Ascorbic Acid):

- **Importance**: Supports immune function, wound healing, and collagen production.

- **Functions:** Vitamin C is essential for the growth and repair of tissues in all parts of your body. It helps the body make collagen which is used to make skin, tendons, ligaments and blood vessels.
- **Benefits:** Acts as an antioxidant protecting cells from damage caused by free radicals. It also boosts the immune system and enhances iron absorption.
- **Examples:** Ascorbic acid
- **Description:** Vitamin C is a water-soluble vitamin that is necessary for normal growth and development.
- **Role in the Body:** It plays a crucial role in wound healing and maintaining healthy skin.
- **Side Effects:** Excessive intake can cause digestive issues such as diarrhea and nausea.

- **Warnings:** Individuals with a history of kidney stones should consult a healthcare professional before taking vitamin C supplements.
- **Precautions:** High doses of vitamin C may interfere with certain laboratory tests.
- **Signs of Deficiency:** Scurvy which includes symptoms like fatigue, inflammation of the gums, joint pain.
- **Amount You Need in the Body:** The recommended dietary allowance (RDA) for vitamin C is 90 milligrams per day for men and 75 milligrams per day for women.
- **Best Way to Consume:** Vitamin C can be obtained from citrus fruits like oranges and lemons as well as from vegetables like bell peppers and broccoli.

Recipe 1:

Orange Juice

Ingredients:
- 2-3 oranges
- Water (optional)
- Honey or sugar (optional)

Instructions:

1. Wash the oranges thoroughly.
2. After peeling the oranges, take out any seeds.
3. Cut the peeled oranges into small pieces.
4. Place the orange pieces in a blender and blend until smooth.
5. If desired, add water to thin the juice and sweeteners like honey or sugar to taste.
6. Blend again until well combined.
7. Serve chilled.

Recipe 2:

Strawberry Smoothie

Ingredients:

- 1 cup strawberries, hulled and frozen
- 1 banana, sliced and frozen
- 1/2 cup orange juice
- 1/2 cup plain yogurt
- 1/2 teaspoon vanilla extract

Instructions:

1. Combine all ingredients in a blender.
2. Blend until smooth and creamy.
3. If the mixture is too thick, add more orange juice or water to thin it out.

4. Taste and adjust sweetness if needed.
5. Serve chilled.

- **Natural Food Sources:**
  - Animal-Based: None
  - Non-Animal Based: Oranges, lemons, bell peppers.

Vitamin D

Vitamin D, also known as the "sunshine vitamin," is essential for preserving general health and wellbeing.

Importance:

1. Bone Health: Vitamin D is essential for the absorption of calcium and phosphorus, which are crucial for maintaining strong and healthy bones. Without an adequate amount of vitamin D, the body is unable to effectively absorb calcium, leading to weakened bones and an increased risk of fractures and bone disorders such as osteoporosis.

2. Immune Function: Vitamin D plays a significant role in supporting the immune system. It helps regulate the function of immune cells and reduces inflammation, thereby contributing to the body's ability to fight off infections and diseases. Adequate levels of vitamin D are associated with a lower risk of autoimmune conditions and respiratory infections.

3. Muscle Function: Maintaining optimal levels of vitamin D is important for muscle strength and function. It supports muscle contraction and movement, making it essential for overall physical performance and reducing the risk of muscle weakness and pain.

4. Mood and Mental Health: There is evidence to suggest that vitamin D may have an impact on mood regulation and mental health. Low levels of vitamin D have been linked to an increased risk of depression, seasonal affective disorder (SAD), and other mood disorders. Adequate vitamin D levels are associated with improved overall well-being.

- **Functions:** Vitamin D helps regulate the amount of calcium and phosphate in the body. To maintain strong bones, teeth, and muscles, these nutrients are necessary.
- **Benefits:** Supports bone health by aiding in calcium absorption. contributes to immunological function as well.

- **Examples:** Ergocalciferol (vitamin D2), cholecalciferol (vitamin D3).
- **Description:** Natural sources of vitamin D are few and low in fat-soluble foods.
- **Role in the Body:** It helps maintain proper levels of calcium and phosphorus in the blood which are essential for bone health.
- **Side Effects:** Excessive intake can lead to high levels of calcium in the blood which can cause nausea and vomiting among other symptoms.
- **Warnings:** Individuals with certain medical conditions or those taking medications should consult a healthcare professional before taking vitamin D supplements.
- **Precautions:** Excessive sun exposure without protection can lead to sunburns or skin damage despite its role in vitamin D synthesis.
- **Signs of Deficiency:** Bone pain or tenderness due to a condition called osteomalacia in adults or rickets in children. Muscle weakness may also occur.
- **Amount You Need in the Body:** The recommended dietary allowance (RDA) for vitamin D is 600 international units (IU) per day for adults up to age 70. For adults over 70 years old it increases to 800 IU per day.
- **Best Way to Consume:** Sunlight triggers the production of vitamin D in the skin but it can

also be obtained from fortified foods such as milk or through supplements.

Recipe

- Sunlight: The human body can produce vitamin D when the skin is exposed to sunlight. Vitamin D is produced by the skin in response to UVB rays from the sun.
- Fatty Fish: Fatty fish such as salmon, mackerel, and tuna are excellent sources of vitamin D.
- Fortified Foods: Many foods are fortified with vitamin D, including milk, orange juice, and some cereals.
- Egg Yolks: Egg yolks contain vitamin D, making them a good dietary source.
- Cod Liver Oil: This supplement is a rich source of vitamin D.

Instructions:

1. Sunlight: Spend time outdoors in sunlight to allow your skin to produce vitamin D naturally.
2. Fatty Fish: Incorporate fatty fish into your diet by grilling, baking, or pan-searing them for a healthy dose of vitamin D.

3. Fortified Foods: Consume fortified foods such as milk, orange juice, and cereals to increase your vitamin D intake.
4. Egg Yolks: Include egg yolks in your meals through dishes like omelets or salads to boost your vitamin D levels.
5. Cod Liver Oil: Take cod liver oil as a dietary supplement to ensure an adequate intake of vitamin D.

Natural Food Sources:
  - Animal-Based: Fatty fish like salmon or mackerel
  - Non-animal Based: Fortified foods such as milk or orange juice.

Vitamin E

  - **Importance:** Supports immune function, healthy skin, and eyesight.
  - **Functions:** Acts as an antioxidant, protects cells from damage, and maintains healthy skin and eyes.
  - **Benefits:** Regulates blood pressure, supports healthy brain function, and reduces the risk of chronic diseases.

- ○ **Examples:** Nuts, seeds, and vegetable oils.
- ○ **Description:** Fat-soluble vitamin required for antioxidant protection and immune function.
- ○ **Role in the body:** Vitamin E is involved in antioxidant protection, immune function, and maintaining healthy skin and eyes.
- ○ **Side effects:** Rare, but excessive intake may cause stomach upset.
- ○ **Warnings:** Deficiency is rare, but it can lead to impaired immune function and poor skin health.
- ○ **Precautions:** No known precautions.
- ○ Signs of deficiency: Impaired immune function and poor skin health.
- ○ **Amount needed in the body:** Adult males require 10 mg/day, females require 8 mg/day.
- ○ **Best way to consume:** Include nuts, seeds, and vegetable oils in the diet.

Vitamin E Rich Recipe: Quinoa Salad with Roasted Vegetables

Quinoa is a nutritious seed that is rich in vitamins, minerals, and antioxidants, including vitamin E. This vitamin E rich recipe combines quinoa with roasted vegetables to create a delicious and healthy dish.

Ingredients

- 1 cup quinoa, rinsed and drained
- 2 cups water or vegetable broth
- 1 red bell pepper, diced
- 1 yellow bell pepper, diced
- 1 small eggplant, diced
- 1 small zucchini, diced
- 1 small red onion, diced
- 3 cloves garlic, minced
- 2 tablespoons olive oil
- Salt and pepper, to taste
- 1/4 cup chopped fresh parsley
- 1/4 cup chopped fresh basil
- 1/4 cup chopped fresh mint
- Two teaspoons of juice from freshly squeezed lemons.

Instructions

1. Preheat the oven to 400°F (200°C).
2. In a large saucepan, combine the quinoa and water or vegetable broth. Once the quinoa is tender and the water has been absorbed, reduce the heat to low, cover, and simmer for 15 to 20 minutes. Turn off the heat and let it to cool.
3. In a large bowl, mix the diced bell peppers, eggplant, zucchini, red onion, and minced garlic. Sprinkle with salt and pepper and drizzle with olive oil. Toss to combine.
4. Spread the vegetable mixture on a baking sheet in a single layer. Roast in the preheated oven for 25-30 minutes, or until the vegetables are tender and slightly browned.
5. In a large mixing bowl, combine the cooked quinoa, roasted vegetables, chopped parsley, basil, mint, and lemon juice. Toss gently to mix well.
6. If necessary, add more salt and pepper to the seasoning. Serve the quinoa salad warm or chilled.

Nutritional Benefits

This vitamin E rich recipe gives a decent wellspring of vitamin E, which is fundamental for keeping up with solid skin, eyes, and invulnerable framework. Additionally, quinoa has a lot of protein, dietary fiber, and a variety of vitamins and minerals. The cooked vegetables add more supplements, including cell reinforcements and fiber.

Natural sources of food: Nuts, seeds, vegetable oils, and entire grains.

Vitamin K

Blood clotting, bone metabolism, and the regulation of blood calcium levels all require vitamin K, a vital nutrient. Remembering vitamin K-rich food varieties for your eating regimen is significant for keeping up with by and large wellbeing.

- **Importance:** Upholds blood coagulating, bone wellbeing, and sound veins.
- **Functions:** Goes about as a cofactor in the blend of proteins engaged with blood thickening.
- **Benefits:** Controls blood coagulating and forestalls over the top dying.

o   **Examples:** Brussels sprouts, broccoli, and other leafy green vegetables

o   **Description:** Fat-solvent nutrient expected for blood thickening and bone wellbeing.

o   **Role in the body:** Proteins needed for blood clotting are synthesized by vitamin K.

o   **Side effects:** Interesting, however extreme admission might cause stomach upset.

o   **Warnings:** A deficiency can result in excessive bleeding and impaired blood clotting. Precautions: No known precautionary measures.

o   **Signs of deficiency:** excessive bleeding and impaired blood clotting

o   **Amount required in the body:** Grown-up guys require 120 mcg/day, females require 90 mcg/day.

Recipe

Incorporate verdant green vegetables, broccoli, and Brussels sprouts in the eating regimen. Recipe: Spinach and Feta Stuffed Chicken Bosom

Ingredients:

- 4 boneless, skinless chicken breasts,
- 2 cups chopped fresh spinach,
- 1/2 cup crumbled feta cheese,
- minced garlic from 2 cloves,
- olive oil,
- dried oregano,
- salt and pepper to taste,

Instructions

1. Preheat the stove to 375°F (190°C).
2. Olive oil should be heated in a skillet over medium heat. Sauté for a minute before adding the minced garlic.
3. Cook until the chopped spinach is wilted in the skillet. Eliminate from intensity and let it cool somewhat.
4. Mix in the disintegrated feta cheddar and dried oregano into the spinach combination. Season with salt and pepper to taste.
5. Pounded each chicken breast to an even thickness between two sheets of plastic wrap.
6. Partition the spinach and feta combination equally among the chicken bosoms, then roll up every chicken bosom, getting with toothpicks if necessary.

7.   Place the stuffed chicken bosoms in a baking dish and prepare for 25-30 minutes or until the chicken is cooked through.

8.   The stuffed chicken breasts should be served with the sides of your choice after the toothpicks have been removed.

In addition to being delicious, this recipe contains a lot of vitamin K from the spinach, making it a healthy addition to your diet.

Normal food sources: whole grains, broccoli, Brussels sprouts, and other leafy green vegetables

MINERALS AND NUTRIENTS

1.   *Calcium:*

• **Importance:** helps muscle function, nerve transmission, and bone health.
• **Functions:** Associated with the arrangement and support of bones and teeth.
• **Benefits:** Manages muscle withdrawals and supports sound heart capability.
○**Examples:** Dairy items, verdant green vegetables, and invigorated grains.
 Description: Mineral needed for healthy teeth and bones, muscle movement, and nerve transmission.
 Role in the body: Calcium is associated with the arrangement and support of bones, teeth, and muscle compressions.
Side effects: Interesting, however extreme admission might cause stomach upset.
○   **Warnings:** Lack can prompt frail bones, muscle squeezes, and debilitated nerve capability.
○   **Precautions:** People with kidney disease may need to cut back on their intake.
○   **Signs of deficiency:** Frail bones, muscle squeezes, and disabled nerve capability.

The amount required by the body: Grown-up guys require 1,000 mg/day, females require 700 mg/day.

o   **Most effective way to consume:** Incorporate dairy items, verdant green vegetables, and braced grains in the eating routine.

Recipe

Calcium-rich recipe - Spinach and ricotta-stuffed entire grain pasta.

Natural food sources: Dairy items, verdant green vegetables, and entire grains.

2. Iron:

o   **Importance:** Supports red blood cell formation and oxygen transport.
o   **Functions:** Involved in the formation of hemoglobin, which carries oxygen in red blood cells.
o   **Benefits:** Regulates energy levels and supports healthy brain function.

- **Examples:** Red meats, poultry, and fortified cereals.
- **Description:** Mineral required for red blood cell formation and oxygen transport.
- **Role in the body:** Iron is involved in the formation of hemoglobin and oxygen transport.
- **Side effects:** Rare, but excessive intake may cause stomach upset.
- **Warnings:** Deficiency can lead to anemia, fatigue, and impaired immune function.
- **Precautions:** Individuals with kidney disease may require reduced intake.
- **Signs of deficiency:** Anemia, fatigue, and impaired immune function.
- **Amount needed in the body:** Adult males require 8 mg/day, females require 18 mg/day.
- **Best way to consume:** Include red meats, poultry, and fortified cereals in the diet.

Recipe

Iron-rich recipe - Grilled chicken with whole-grain pasta and fortified cereal.

- **Natural food sources:** Red meats, poultry, fortified cereals, and whole grains.

Magnesium:

- **Importance:** Supports muscle and nerve function, energy production, and bone health.
- **Functions:** Involved in over 300 enzyme reactions, including energy metabolism.
- **Benefits:** Regulates muscle and nerve function, blood sugar levels, and blood pressure.
- **Examples:** Nuts, seeds, and leafy green vegetables.
- **Description:** Mineral required for energy production, muscle and nerve function, and bone health.
- **Role in the body:** Magnesium is involved in over 300 enzyme reactions, including energy metabolism.
- **Side effects:** Rare, but excessive intake may cause stomach upset.

- **Warnings:** Deficiency can lead to muscle cramps, fatigue, and impaired nerve function.
- **Precautions:** No known precautions.
- **Signs of deficiency:** Muscle cramps, fatigue, and impaired nerve function.
- **Amount needed in the body:** Adult males require 400 mg/day, females require 310 mg/day.
- **Best way to consume:** Include nuts, seeds, and leafy green vegetables in the diet.

Recipe

Magnesium-rich recipe - Almond-crusted salmon with whole-grain rice and vegetables.

- **Natural food sources:** Nuts, seeds, leafy green vegetables, and whole grains.

Phosphorus:

- **Importance:** Supports bone health, energy production, and cellular function.
- **Functions:** Involved in the formation of ATP, the body's primary energy source.

- **Benefits:** Regulates energy levels, supports healthy brain function, and maintains bone strength.
- **Examples:** Dairy products, meats, and fortified cereals.
- **Description:** Mineral required for energy production, bone health, and cellular function.
- **Role in the body:** Phosphorus is involved in the formation of ATP, the body's primary energy source.
- **Side effects:** Rare, but excessive intake may cause stomach upset.
- **Warnings:** Deficiency is rare, but it can lead to weak bones and impaired energy production.
- **Precautions:** No known precautions.
- **Signs of deficiency:** Weak bones and impaired energy production.
- **Amount needed in the body:** Adult males require 700 mg/day, females require 700 mg/day.
- **Best way to consume:** Include dairy products, meats, and fortified cereals in the diet.

- **Phosphorus-rich recipe** - Grilled chicken with whole-grain pasta and fortified cereal.
- **Natural food sources:** Dairy products, meats, fortified cereals, and whole grains.

Potassium

- **Importance:** Supports muscle and nerve function, fluid balance, and blood pressure regulation.
- **Functions:** Involved in maintaining fluid balance and regulating blood pressure.
- **Benefits:** Regulates muscle contractions, nerve transmission, and supports healthy heart function.
- **Examples:** Bananas, potatoes, and leafy green vegetables.
- **Description:** Mineral required for muscle and nerve function, fluid balance, and blood pressure regulation.
- **Role in the body:** Potassium is involved in maintaining fluid balance and regulating blood pressure.

- **Side effects:** Rare, but excessive intake may cause stomach upset.
- **Warnings:** Deficiency can lead to muscle cramps, fatigue, and impaired nerve function.
- **Precautions:** No known precautions.
- **Signs of deficiency:** Muscle cramps, fatigue, and impaired nerve function.
- **Amount needed in the body:** Adult males require 3,800 mg/day, females require 2,700 mg/day.
- **Best way to consume:** Include bananas, potatoes, and leafy green vegetables in the diet.

Recipe

- **Potassium-rich recipe** - Banana and spinach smoothie with whole-grain toast.
- **Natural food sources:** Bananas, potatoes, leafy green vegetables, and whole grains.

Sodium

- **Importance:** Supports fluid balance, nerve function, and muscle contractions.
- **Functions:** Involved in maintaining fluid balance and regulating blood pressure.
- **Benefits:** Regulates muscle contractions, nerve transmission, and supports healthy heart function.
- **Examples:** Salt, processed foods, and dairy products.
- **Description:** Mineral required for fluid balance, nerve function, and muscle contractions.
- **Role in the body:** Sodium is involved in maintaining fluid balance and regulating blood pressure.
- **Side effects:** Rare, but excessive intake may cause stomach upset.
- **Warnings:** Deficiency is rare, but it can lead to muscle cramps, fatigue, and impaired nerve function.
- **Precautions:** No known precautions.
- **Signs of deficiency:** Muscle cramps, fatigue, and impaired nerve function.

- **Amount needed in the body:** Adult males require 1,500 mg/day, females require 1,500 mg/day.
- **Best way to consume:** Include salt, processed foods, and dairy products in the diet.

Recipe

- **Sodium-rich recipe** - Grilled chicken with whole-grain pasta and fortified cereal.
- **Natural food sources:** Salt, processed foods, and whole grains.

Zinc:
- **Importance:** Supports immune function, protein synthesis, and cell division.
- **Functions:** Involved in over 300 enzyme reactions, including protein synthesis.
- **Benefits:** Regulates immune function, growth, and reproductive health.
- **Examples:** Oysters, red meats, and fortified cereals.

- **Description:** Mineral required for immune function, protein synthesis, and cell division.
- **Role in the body:** Zinc is involved in over 300 enzyme reactions, including protein synthesis.
- **Side effects:** Rare, but excessive intake may cause stomach upset.
- **Warnings:** Deficiency can lead to impaired immune function, slow wound healing, and poor growth.
- **Precautions:** No known precautions.
- Signs of deficiency: Impaired immune function, slow wound healing, and poor growth.
- **Amount needed in the body:** Adult males require 11 mg/day, females require 8 mg/day.
- **Best way to consume:** Include oysters, red meats, and fortified cereals in the diet.

Recipe

- **Zinc-rich recipe** - Oyster and spinach stir-fry with whole-grain rice.

- ○ **Natural food sources:** Oysters, red meats, fortified cereals, and whole grains.

CONCLUSION

In conclusion, the impacts of nutrients on health are vast and varied. A balanced diet, rich in macronutrients and micronutrients, is essential for maintaining good health and preventing chronic diseases. By understanding the importance of each nutrient and consuming a diverse range of foods, individuals can ensure they are providing their body with the essential nutrients it needs to function optimally.